ESTONIAN MYTHOLOGY & LEGENDS

Hourly Journey Through Time with Myth

CHRONICLE PRESS

Hourly Myth Journey

Set out on an hourly myth journey! Dive into captivating stories based on old mythology that were carefully written so you can finish reading them in an hour. Our carefully chosen collection lets you unleash the power of famous stories. Each page opens up a world of gods, heroes, creatures and timeless wonders. In just 60 minutes, you can spark your mind, enjoy the magic, and escape into worlds that come to life. Mythology meets speed, and you'll find the joy of an epic story in each quick part. Get better at reading one story at a time because legends are waiting, and time is running out!

Copyright © 2024

Copyright © 2024

Disclaimer

The author is solely responsible for this book's information, ideas, and opinions; they do not necessarily represent the views of any institutions or individuals associated with the author. The author has made what they believe to be reasonable steps to make sure that the material contained in this book is accurate. However, neither the author nor the publisher makes any representations or guarantees, either stated or implied, regarding the completeness, accuracy, reliability, appropriateness, or availability of the content contained within. It is strongly recommended that readers seek assistance from relevant professionals or specialists in specific disciplines by consulting with them to acquire precise information tailored to their particular situations. The author disclaims liability for any loss, damage, or harm resulting from using the information provided in this book and any omissions or errors.

This book may reference websites, goods, services, or resources owned or operated by third parties. These references are solely offered for your convenience, and their inclusion does not indicate that we approve, sponsor, or recommend the content provided by the third party. Because the author and the publisher do not have any control over the nature, content, or availability of external websites, they cannot be held liable for any actions, decisions, or consequences resulting from using such external resources.

Forward

I would want to extend an invitation to go on a voyage that is genuinely extraordinary to those of you who are interested in unearthing ancient knowledge, who are captivated by the mysterious stories that are woven through the fabric of human life, and who are aficionados of the rich tapestry of mythology that transcends boundaries and resonates across time. Within this book's covers, we will explore the halls of myth and completely submerge ourselves in the ageless tales that have enthralled the human imagination for as long as anybody can remember.

In all of its magnificence, mythology acts as a compass that directs us through the complexities of the human experience. It is a mirror that reflects our perception of the universe and our role and embodies our collective dreams, fears, goals, and ideals. Mythology invites us to investigate the hidden aspects of our lives, whether we are more interested in the sweeping conflicts between gods and heroes or the hidden meanings in the stories of how the world was created.

Within these pages, you will encounter many pantheons and deities, each providing a distinctive perspective to examine the more expansive universe. It is essential to remember that mythology is not only a relic of the past but a living phenomenon that continues to impact our contemporary reality. Its influence can be seen in literature, art, music, and daily language. It invigorates us, sparks the fire of our imagination, and gives us a glimpse into the intricate web that is the history of humanity.

Mythology also acts as a connector, bringing together people from different cultures worldwide. It brings us together by highlighting the similarities in our experiences and the uniqueness of each of us as individuals. In the vast Pantheon of mythical figures, we find examples of universal themes such as love, betrayal, heroism, and sacrifice. These themes connect with every human heart, regardless of when or where they were written.

This book is both a celebration of mythology and an invitation to go on an adventure of discovery. This is an homage to the innumerable storytellers who have ensured the survival of these myths through the ebb and flow of the sands of time by passing them down from generation to generation. It is devoted to all people interested in mythology, namely those who find comfort in the ageless stories that have shaped our world since the beginning of time and continue to do so Today.

Therefore, I implore you, dear reader, to turn the page and completely submerge yourself in the enthralling delights that are still to come. Let us all come together to celebrate the mythology that brings us together, is not limited by the constraints of culture or time, and imparts a feeling of awe and wonder into our everyday lives.

Your imagination will be stoked, your horizons will be expanded, and you will be reminded of the eternal power of storytelling if you allow yourself to go on this voyage into the realms of mythology. And may you emerge from these pages, like the heroes of old, changed by the insight and enchantment that mythology has to give due to what you've learned here.

TABLE OF CONTENTS

Introduction

The term "Estonian mythology" refers to a collection of legends and fables passed down from generation to generation among the Estonian people before the arrival of colonizers. Not many documents of this mythology have been preserved because the norm of passing on Estonian beliefs from one generation to the next was done verbally. On the other hand, it is possible to assert, based on certain narratives that have been preserved up until the present day, that the original myth of the Estonian people was founded on the amalgamation of religions shared by the Finno-Baltic and Finno-Ugric tribes, which resulted in a wide variety of myths and sacred writings.

Since the 13th century, the dominance of Estonia's conquerors has significantly impacted Estonian mythology. As a result, relatively few recordings of Estonian beliefs date back to the time period before that. The reason for this is that the Estonian people have a long-standing practice of passing down their original beliefs and customs from one generation to the next through oral tradition. This continued until the entrance of outsiders, who brought their own culture to the Estonian people and subjected them to it through violent means.

Because they were regarded as "pagan" people, they were coerced into becoming Christians. Nevertheless, it is possible to assert that Estonian myth is founded on natural deities, given the limited number of narratives preserved over time. The thunder god Pikne, sometimes known as "Pikker," is one of the most significant deities during the pre-Christian era. This god is intimately connected to the myth of Kreutzwald, the supreme deity, playing "Pikker's trumpet."

The unity of all the peoples that came to the Baltic beaches is reflected in the mythology of ancient Estonia. This union is primarily portrayed in the folklore of the Estonian people, which has been influenced by the culture and the Finno-Ugric and Balto-Finnish individuals over more than a thousand years. The "runo songs" collected by the Estonian people preceding their conquerors' arrival contain ancient myths passed down from generation to generation. Among these are the myths that date back to the beginning of Estonian mythology.

In one of these tunes, the world's origin is discussed in Estonian mythology. According to Estonian mythology, the Finno-Ugric peoples and Estonians believe that the world originated from an egg from which it emerged. A universe from where their forefathers originated is another topic that they discuss.

There was a mystical tree that represented the universe of the ancestors. The Milky Way was one of the branches of this tree, and as a result, existence was divided. As a result of the cultural interchange that took place among the Estonian population and the Baltic or Germanic nations, the beliefs that reside within Estonian mythology underwent a period of transformation.

This marked the beginning of the representations of higher deities directly related to nature. It was especially prevalent in rural areas, where Estonian farmers lived, where they strongly believed in the gods of climate and fertility. In addition, some songs are mystical, such as those that talk about giants, natural occurrences or phenomena that cannot be explained, and meteorites that landed on Estonian land thousands of years ago.

Many different stories from Estonian folklore and literature make up Estonian mythology. In runic songs, you might be able to find traces of the oldest real stories. A song says that the world was born when a bird laid three eggs and began to spread them out. One of the eggs became the Sun, one became the Moon, and one became the Earth. There are also stories among other Finno-Ugric groups that say the world came from an egg. For Estonian ancestors, the world seemed to revolve around a column or tree, and the North Star seemed nailed to the sky.

Estonia is linked to the bird cultures of the past and pre-ancient female tribal magic worldwide through the Milky Way. Their inductee is a part of the world tree or how birds move. The ideas in these stories came from shamanistic rites, practices, and beliefs. As the proto-Estonian people lived in touch with Germanic tribes and switched from gathering and hunting to farming, their mythology changed.

Sky and weather gods and fertility gods and gods of the sky and weather became important to farmers. A god of the sky and thunder might have been named Uku or Ukko. He was also known as Vanaisa or Taevataat. A sky god named Jumal may have been one of the pre-Christian gods of Proto-Estonian people. This god is also known as Jumala in Finnish and Jumo in Mari.

Estonian stories about giants might have come from

Germanic cultures. Many stories say that different natural features and items are signs of Kalevipoeg's deeds. The giant and the Christian Devil have joined together to form a new figure called Vanapagan. He is a giant demon who lives on his farm or manor with his farm hand, Kaval-Ants—the Tuhala Witch's Well and old Estonian stories. Over the years, Estonia has had many different religions, from Catholicism and Lutheranism to Russian Orthodoxy and Soviet communism.

Estonia is one of the world's most secular countries; in the census conducted in 2011, only 20% of its citizens said they were religious. This is 22 years after Estonia gained freedom from the Soviet Union. But most Estonians still feel a strong, sometimes mythical, link to nature. Estonians first heard about Christianity when German merchants came to the country in the late 1200s and brought Christian preachers. Their task didn't go as planned because Estonians were against an outside religion. The Christian crusaders took about a hundred years to take over the country. They forced the people to become Christians, which was the start of a long time when other nations ruled Estonia.

But Estonians weren't completely without faith in the time before Christianity. Animal-based faiths like Taaraism and Maausk interested them. Their god was out in the wild. People in Estonia are quick to cast aside modern religions. However, beliefs from the past like these are nevertheless a big part of Estonian society.

During the long time that other countries controlled Estonia, old ideas lived on in the form of folk tales. For example, in stories, lakes fly away as punishment when greedy villages or forests leave in the middle of the night and never return. Leaves on trees expect to be tipped, and coins must be put in holes in the ground.

One of these old folk tales is shown in Tuhala Witches' Well. The Tuhala settlement is thought to be over three thousand years old. It is located in Estonia's largest area of porous karst. Fifteen underground rivers run through a maze of caves, making noises that people can hear but not see. These changes have caused sinkholes big enough to swallow horses.

When too much water in the Mahtra swamp fills the underground river, it tries to escape through the well. This is what happens at Tuhala Witch's Well. Water starts to shoot up from the hole and flood the area. At least 5,000 litres of water must move along the Tuhala River every second for it to go over. It doesn't happen every year; the water only comes out for a short time. It often takes place in late March and early April.

Gods & Goddess

In Estonian folklore, gods and goddesses are often linked to different parts of nature, people's activities, and general ideas. They are the things that make the world and people's lives what they are. People worship, fear, and sometimes make peace with these gods through rites and gifts. There are gods and goddesses in the Pantheon who are in charge of things in nature, like the sun, moon, stars, sky, earth, water, and woods. People often make them into people and honour them as gods with power over their areas.

Along with gods connected to natural things, there are also gods connected to human actions and ideas, like farming, making things, war, fertility, wisdom, love, and children. People think these gods and goddesses affect human affairs and can help, protect, or even challenge people and groups. Legendary heroes in many Estonian myths may not be gods in the traditional sense. However, they have amazing powers and are important in shaping the mythological story. Often, these heroes go on quests, fight mythical creatures, and show bravery, wisdom, and other traits that are important to society.

Taara: The supreme god in Estonian mythology

The god Taara is a significant figure in Estonian mythology. He shares many parallels with the deity Ukko, from Finland, and the god Thor, from Germany. The Oeselians, in particular, believed that Taara was the most powerful deity in the Estonian Pantheon. Several people have suggested that "Tharapita" can be read as "Taara, help!"

There is a lack of clarity regarding the origins of Taara; however, the name may be connected to the Livonian location named "Thoreyda," which might be read to mean "garden of Taara for Thor." With this information, it appears that the name Taara was popular among the inhabitants of Livonian. Various Uralic and German deities, including the Khanty deity Torum, the Sami deity Turms, or the Samoyedic god Tere, have been linked to Taara. Taara has also been shown to be affiliated with other deities. Turisas, the god of Finland, has also been connected to Taara in some circles.

In the Chronicle of Henry of Livonia, written in the thirteenth century, Tharapita is described as the superior god of the Oeselians. Additionally, the

Vironian tribe in northern Estonia were familiar with Tharapita. According to the chronicle, the people who lived in the area believed that Tharapita was born on a hill in Vironia covered with gorgeous forests. From there, he travelled by flying to the volcanic island of Saaremaa. On Thursdays, sometimes referred to as "evenings of Tooru," it was stated that Estonians did not work. Over several evenings, people would congregate in sacred groves, where a piper musician would sit on the ground and play while others danced and chanted till morning.

During the middle of the 19th century, the Taara turned into a well-known symbol of the Estonian national movement. It was utilized as a sign of opposition to both Germans and Lutherans. Tartu was called the "Taaralinn" or the "city of Taara" throughout this period because of its lyrical significance. According to the Estonian neopagan trend known as "taaralased" or "taarausulized," Taara was also the inspiration for this movement. On the other hand, several academics contend that the contemporary portrayal of Taara as the ultimate creator of Estonia resulted from pseudo mythology that originated in the 19th century rather than representing the genuine historical significance of the deity.

Peko: Estonian God of Fertility

One of the most prominent deities in Estonian folklore and mythology is Peko, according to the search results that were offered. Peko is a deity associated with agriculture who was thought to promote the development of crops, particularly barley, and to bring good fortune to households. In ancient times, he was revered as a god of brewing and fertility.

Peko was symbolized by a wax figure buried in the grain during the granary as part of a ceremony to boost agricultural production. This image was pulled out in the early Spring for the ritual. An ethnic minority in Estonia known as the Seto people would go to the statue known as "Peko" before attempting significant endeavours to pray for good fortune and prosperity, and they would also make sacrifices there.

Peko is a character deeply associated with the brewing process and barley in the mythology of Estonia and Finland. He was believed to be a god who could ensure a plentiful harvest and guarantee that the land would be fertile. There is a possibility that the name "Peko" is derived from the Estonian word "pekk," which may be translated as "fat" or "lard." This would imply that the name is associated with agricultural plenty and success.

In the mythology of Finland, Peko is also called "Pellon-Peko" on occasion. Some academics claim that the present depiction of Peko as a supreme deity could result from nationalism and pseudo mythology from the 19th century rather than reflecting his genuine historical significance. This is despite Peko being a significant character in traditional Estonian or Seto beliefs.

Maa-ema: Goddess of Mother Earth

Maa-ema, often spelt May-emma, is a major part of Estonian mythology. She is a representation of Mother Earth to the Estonian people. She is venerated because she is a symbol of the aspect of the earth that is responsible for providing nourishment and life. Maa-ema is a figure related to the planet concept as a maternal figure in Estonian pseudomythology. She is said to embody conception, growth, and sustenance.

This goddess is a member of the mythology of Estonian deities, where she is revered for her position as the personification of the land and the abundance that it provides. It is common practice to picture Maa-ema as a source of life, one accountable for the blossoming of flowers and the abundant fertility of the ground. Her inclusion in Estonian folklore draws attention to the profound link between the people of Estonia.

The significance of Maa-ema extends beyond the realm of mythological stories; it is resonant with societal beliefs and actions that revere the land as a supplier and a sustainer of life. To show their respect for Maa-ema and acknowledge her role in maintaining the equilibrium and harmony of the natural world, Estonians perform rituals, tell stories, and use symbols. Maa-ema is a cherished person in Estonian culture because she embodies the spirit of Mother Earth and the relationship between humans and the environment. In essence, she is a revered figure.

Vanemuine: God of Creativity

Musicians and poets find inspiration in Vanemuine, the God of Creativity. Those creative in Estonia are believed to feel a resonance in their hearts when they hear his music. Within the realm of Estonian mythology, Vanemuine is a god. Estonian mythology was developed in the 19th century by Friedrich Robert Faehlmann and Friedrich Reinhold Kreutzwald. The god of melodies, art, and literature is known as Vanemuine.

Within this manufactured Estonian mythology framework, Vanemuine is regarded as the deity of songs, art, and literature. "Eldermost" and "Eldest" are terms occasionally used to refer to him. The concept of Vanemuine was not a part of the genuine pre-Christian Estonian mythology; rather, it was a part of the nationalist effort in the 19th century to establish a mythological tradition for Estonia.

It is most possible that the Swedish legendary figure Vainamoinen was the source of inspiration for the character of Vanemuine. To summarize, Vanemuine is a male deity, not a goddess, created as part of the development of Estonian national mythology in the

19th century. Rather than being part of the genuine pre-Christian Estonian belief system, Vanemuine was created as part of building an Estonian national mythology.

Mythical Creatures

In Estonian mythology, many different kinds of mythical animals live in nature. Each one has its special traits and meaning. These beings often blur the lines between the physical and spiritual worlds by having natural and supernatural skills. Estonian mythology is full of animals representing the people's cultural values, beliefs, and world views. These creatures help us understand how they relate to nature and the mysteries of life. There are many stories about these creatures in folklore. They shape the mythological landscape and make people think, be amazed, and be curious.

Estonian folklore has a lot to do with nature. Many creatures in the stories are spirits or guardians of certain natural features, like forests, mountains, and lakes. People think these spirits live in the land and can show up in various forms, from friendly guardians to sneaky pranksters. In Estonian mythology, there are many different kinds of magical animals.

Shape-shifting creatures that can change their appearance at will are popular in Estonian folklore. They can often move between planets or realms and look like people, animals, or other things. People who can change their shape may have magical skills and appear in mythological stories in good and bad ways. In Estonian mythology, some creatures act as guardians or defenders of certain places, things, or people. People usually think of these beings as strong and scary allies that protect against evil forces or help travellers on their travels.

Metsik the Forest Guardian

When it comes to the forest, Metsik is the elf. According to ancient Estonian stories, the Metsik were wood elves that inhabited wherever surrounded by trees, from the shallow swamp forests to the dense coniferous woodlands. Metsik reveals themselves to people as a wild animal, a bird, or a gorgeous tree when they appear. The songs that a singing bird, a Metsik, sings are ones humans can comprehend. In addition, they can comprehend the language of the aspen tree, Metsik, the language of the poplar tree that rustles in the wind.

Metsik may be the bird that is singing for people when they hear the sound of a bird singing. Those near an aspen tree rustling in the wind can hear Metsik. They oppose dumping rubbish, starting fires, and cutting down trees. If individuals enter the woods with ill will in their hearts, Metsik will direct them away from their sacred property. It is said that Metsik is the spirit that watches over the forests. They oppose cutting down trees, starting fires, and, most importantly, trashing. When someone visits the woods to cause harm, Metsik leads them astray, causing them to depart from their holy dwelling.

Allikaravitseja The Healing Waters

She is a spirit of healing who resides in the hot springs, and her name is Allikaravitseja. In addition, there is a significant quantity of sand present in the boiling waters, which has the potential to form a shape that resembles a human body. The reflections of the neighbouring trees and bushes have the potential to shape themselves into human shapes as well.

The spirit manifests itself in the presence of those carrying out a ceremony. They toss a coin into the Spring to determine what they are concerned about. Another thing that makes the Spirit of the Spring happy is when fragments of silver are left behind as a sacrifice. Even though Allikaravitseja is not very forthcoming with her identity, her voice can be heard, reminiscent of a whisper emanating from the ocean.

Asking Allikaravitseja for guidance is something that anybody can do. While tossing a coin into the

Spring, you should name your problem. When you make a sacrifice comprised of bits of silver, she is delighted with you. There are just a few instances in which Allikaravitseja is seen. However, her voice may be heard from the water, barely audible.

Maausk: Invisible Sprit

"Maausk" refers to a group of pagan beliefs that are traditional to Estonia. These beliefs include the belief in unseen spirits, predecessors, the magical animals mentioned above, and old rituals and magic. In indigenous religion, "Maausk" is a broad concept encompassing grassroots groups that worship the local gods and environment. It is primarily the Estonian pagan confederation Maavalla Koda that is responsible for the administration of the movement.

One of the last regions to be converted to Christianity was the Baltic region, which includes the Baltic countries. The continuation of pagan beliefs in the region might also be attributed to this factor. It is also stated that Estonia has the country with the largest population of atheists of any country in the world.

A polytheistic or pantheistic belief in the earth itself was the primary impetus behind the Maausk movement, which emerged. Jõulud, the winter solstice, and Jaanipäev, the summer solstice, are the two holidays that hold the most significance in the calendar.

Regularly, followers of Maausk travel to holy sites in Hiis. These features include stone formations, glacial boulders, ancient trees, and bodies of water. There may be a sauna, a fireplace, or a swing in the vicinity of the shrine. The purpose of people going to the shrines is to obtain spiritual calm and to develop harmony with nature around them.

Hiid, The Giant

The word "Hiid" can be interpreted differently in Estonian. The term "Hiid" can refer to a sacred grove or an ancient pagan place of worship in the natural environment. In addition to this, Hiid is a king or a spirit that protects sacred vegetation. They have a low, deep voice and can communicate all of the languages humans, trees, and animals speak.

They are giant-sized elves. Hiid can transform into

various forms, including a mountain, a high tree, or a bull elk. Hiid can doze off for several years and transform into a hill at certain times. It was a massive boulder that no one ever recognized that roused him from his sleep.

Soovana: The Saddened Mist

The protector of wetland areas is a spirit known as Soovana. Amid the fog or a swamp, he materializes. At times, the mist takes on peculiar forms, which most likely served as the source of inspiration for the legend of Soovana. Soovana may have cranberries sprouting in his hair if the bog turf contains an unusually high number of cranberries. When he is experiencing bouts of grief and depression, even picking cranberries may cause him to become angry. It is important to avoid disturbing him because of this.

Kivialune: The Cave Spirit

The spirit known as Kivialune is a diminutive being who resides and meditates in caves made of stone. Because he enjoys being alone, he may remain still and quiet for days. When it's all said and done, he emerges into his environment. He continues to dwell in the most obscure section of the stone cave. Kivialune sends a giant stone roll down on his location to get rid of any unwelcome intruders that may be around. He has no intention of causing harm to the unwelcome visitor. The only thing he wants to do is scare them.

Saarevaht: The Islander

The guardian of the islands is known as Saarevaht. He has a connection with the ocean and rivers. There are secluded locations where Saarevaht finds himself. More often than not, he is the ghost that guards the lighthouse. In addition to turning himself into a fox or an eagle, he can converse with plants. He has a kind and peaceful spirit and takes pleasure in guiding tourists around the island where he was born. His anger is fueled by carelessness and harshness. He is irritated by behaviour that is both sloppy and impolite.

Murumem: Guardian Sprit

The Murumen is said to be the spirit that watches over the fields and farmlands. Because she is very concerned about the earth's health, she offers information to other people interested in the earth, which has been around for centuries. Murumemm takes pleasure in working in nature and overseeing the upkeep of the property. As the bees hold a special place in her heart, she cares for them. "Murumemm is a joyful person who has a passion for dancing."

Legends and Folklore

The mythology of Estonia comprises many tales and stories that have been told orally from generation to generation. These stories cover many different topics, such as how the world came to be, the adventures of famous heroes, the relationships between gods and humans, and the reasons behind natural events. Here are some general ideas about Estonian mythology tales and folklore. Creation stories in Estonian mythology explain how the world and all the people who live in it came to be. Often, gods or supernatural forces shape the world, the earth, and the different realms where gods, spirits, and humans live in these myths.

In Estonian folklore, epic stories are very common. They tell of the adventures and triumphs of legendary heroes who go on quests, fight mythical creatures, and overcome difficult challenges. These heroes show the values and qualities important to the culture, like bravery, honour, wisdom, and toughness. Folklore in Estonia is full of stories and myths that teach lessons, entertain, and give us insight into what it means to be human. In these stories, talking animals, cunning trolls, wise old people, and other classic characters who deal with the complicated issues of life and society may be present. Folktales and legends from Estonian mythology can help you understand how the people there think about the beginning of life, death, and the future. Often, these stories ask existential questions about what it means to be alive and the world's mysteries.

Kalevipoeg

According to Estonian tales, Kalevipoeg would carry or throw stones at his adversaries. In addition, he will utilize planks that are edgewise as weapons, as he was instructed to do by a hedgehog. Additionally, he constructs towns and makes surface structures on the landscape or bodies of water with his hands. He navigates his way through the water. Eventually, Kalevipoeg passes away as a result of his own feet being severed by his sword. This was a consequence of his previous instructions, which were fatally vague.

Kalevipoeg is the youngest child of Kalev and Linda. He was born after his father died away, and he outperformed his brothers regarding intelligence and power. It is a common misconception that Sohni or Soini was Kalevipoeg's real name; however, the literal meaning of Sohni or Soini is "son," and any other title than Kalevipoeg has never known him. His family had three brothers: Alevipoeg, Olevipoeg, and Sulevipoeg.

Most of the content comes from Estonian folklore, specifically from the story of a huge hero named Kalevipoeg. Most of these stories interpret various natural objects and characteristics as traces of

Kalevipoeg's acts. Additionally, these stories share commonalities with national epic tales from neighbouring regions, particularly the Finnish Kalevala.

To locate his mother, Kalevipoeg embarks on a journey to Finland. He acquires a sword during his travels, but amid an argument, he kills the Blacksmith's oldest son. The sword is cursed by the Blacksmith who forged it before. Suppose Kalevipoeg triumphs over his siblings in a competition involving stone-throwing. In that case, he is crowned king upon his return to Estonia. In Estonia, he works the land and constructs towns and forts. Kalevipoeg then embarks on a trek to the end of the world to broaden his understanding. Through a test of strength, Jesus triumphs over Satan and saves three young women from the depths of hell.

During the outbreak of war, Estonia is subjected to destruction. After Kalevipoeg's loyal allies die, he passes the throne to the younger Olev. He retreats to the woods, where he becomes melancholy. The sword cursed by the Blacksmith and lost in the river attacks him while he is crossing a river and slices off both of his legs. After passing away, Kalevipoeg is taken to paradise. After consulting with the other gods, Taara reanimates Kalevipoeg, mounts his legless body on a white stallion, and then sends him below to the gates of hell. Once there, he is given the order to smash the rock with his fist, resulting in hell being trapped inside the rock. As a result, Kalevipoeg continues to watch over the entrances to hell.

Kalevipoeg has been mentioned in a variety of contexts, including formal institutions as well as popular culture. After the main character's death, Kalevipoeg, the Estonian statement of Independence opens with a paragraph that quotes a god from Canto XX. This verse comes immediately after the fact.

The Devil's Wedding

According to this urban legend, an extremely wealthy guy from Estonia is said to have thrown away all of his wealth. At the time when he was on the edge of becoming bankrupt and taking his own life, a very odd person visited him at his home and offered to provide him with all of his riches back and more on the condition that he fulfilled a certain requirement.

To throw a party, he was required to grant permission to that peculiar individual to use the upstairs floor of his home for a single night. On the other hand, he warned him that he would take his own life if those around him were unable to see what was transpiring there.

The wealthy man accepted the offer, eager to regain his fortune. The house was empty when the party was over, and the affluent individual regained his wealth and continued wasting it. However, during the early morning hours, his butler passed away. Before his death, he admitted to the priest of the town that he had witnessed the party being a celebration of "the devil's wedding."

Marzipan: Local Legend

It is also known as the "Mart's Bread" legend. It tells the narrative of how, according to the ideas of Estonian mythology, the syrupy combination of almond candy and sugar is said to have originated from this region. The pharmacy in the city hall square in Tallinn, Estonia, is the location in question.

When the town councilman could not locate a treatment for his ailment, he went to the lone pharmacy in town. The apothecary ordered his apprentice pharmacist, Mart, to produce the medicine. This is when everything began.

While producing the concoction, Mart substituted the bitter components with sweet tastes. After taking it, the councilman saw an improvement in his health. He was so pleased with the flavour that he ordered it to be manufactured in large quantities. As a result, the remedy gained widespread recognition in Estonia and was sometimes referred to as "Mardileib" or "Mart's bread."

Old Lake Ülemiste

This is the story of an elderly guy known as "Ülemiste Vanake" who resides in the Lake around Tallinn. During the fall season, it is believed that he travels from house to house in the village to inquire about whether or not the village has been finished or whether any building needs to be finished.

The elderly Ulemiste walks to the Lake in peace after receiving the response that it is not yet ready, and he does not return until the autumn of the next year. If, on the other hand, they respond in the affirmative, then the old man will, following the ideas established in Estonian mythology, flood the hamlet with the waters of the Lake.

Old Thomas

During ancient times in Estonia, it was a tradition to hold a competition using bows and arrows. The competition consisted of hanging a carved parrot on the highest point of a hill, and the winner was the person who could bring it down.

However, participation was restricted to members of Estonian aristocratic houses. But a young lad went by the name "Tomas." He was full of bravery, and because he was the only person with experience with the bow and arrow, he ventured to participate in the competition. He was the only one who was successful in bringing the parrot down.

Because Tomas was afraid he might get arrested for his bravery, he ran away. However, it turned out that he was selected as an apprentice guard due to his skills. It was a complete surprise to everyone that he became the best warrior; his exploits during the Livonian conflict left an indelible impact on the history of Estonian legend.

One Last Thing...

We're glad you're interested in this book. I hope you have as much fun reading it as I did writing it. This book is for all those people with big eyes and many questions. I hope your interest in these old stories will help them live on forever.

I have always considered your insightful reviews to be an excellent source of viewpoints on books, and it would be an honour for me if you would review This book. Your perceptive analysis and comments would not only be of great use to me as an author, but they would also serve potential readers in understanding the issues and traits covered in the book. I am very aware of the constraints imposed by the little time you have at your disposal; thus, I ask that you please consider the following request.

I am thankful that you considered what I had to say about the book and took the time to do so. I would be more than happy to provide some further input and ideas. Please do not hesitate to contact me. If you would like to give feedback on my book, you only need to navigate to the reviews part of my content. You will notice a sizable button that asks you to "Write a customer review." Select that link, and you will be taken to the appropriate page.

Made in the USA
Las Vegas, NV
02 December 2024

13215623R00024